Words **Joel Rickett**
Pictures **Spencer Wilson**

ModernABC.com
facebook.com/modernabc

Q

is for Quinoa

• A Modern Parent's ABC •

The Overlook Press
New York, NY

For Sophie, Esme, Gracie and Isla,
who finish all their quinoa–sometimes.

Au pair

Apple sauce

App

Bb

Babiators

Baby carrier

Babymoon

Baby yoga

Baby proof

Cc

Cloth diapers

Dd

Drama

Daycare

Equipped (for everything)

Earplugs

Edamame

Ee

F R I D G E

Expecting

Flash cards

happy

sad

Floorbed

F f

Facepaint

Formula

Glamping

Guilt

Gg

Growth spurt

Hummus

Happy Puffs

Hooter hiders

Hunter boots

Hh

Helicopter parenting

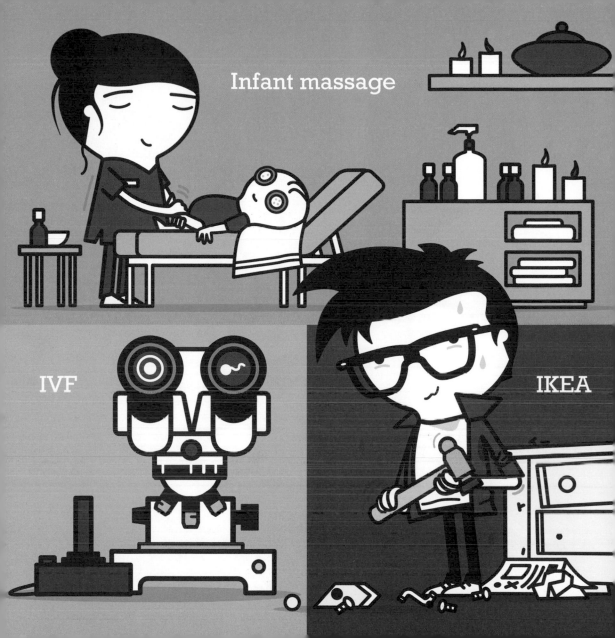

Jj

Jiu jitsu

Joggin' stroller

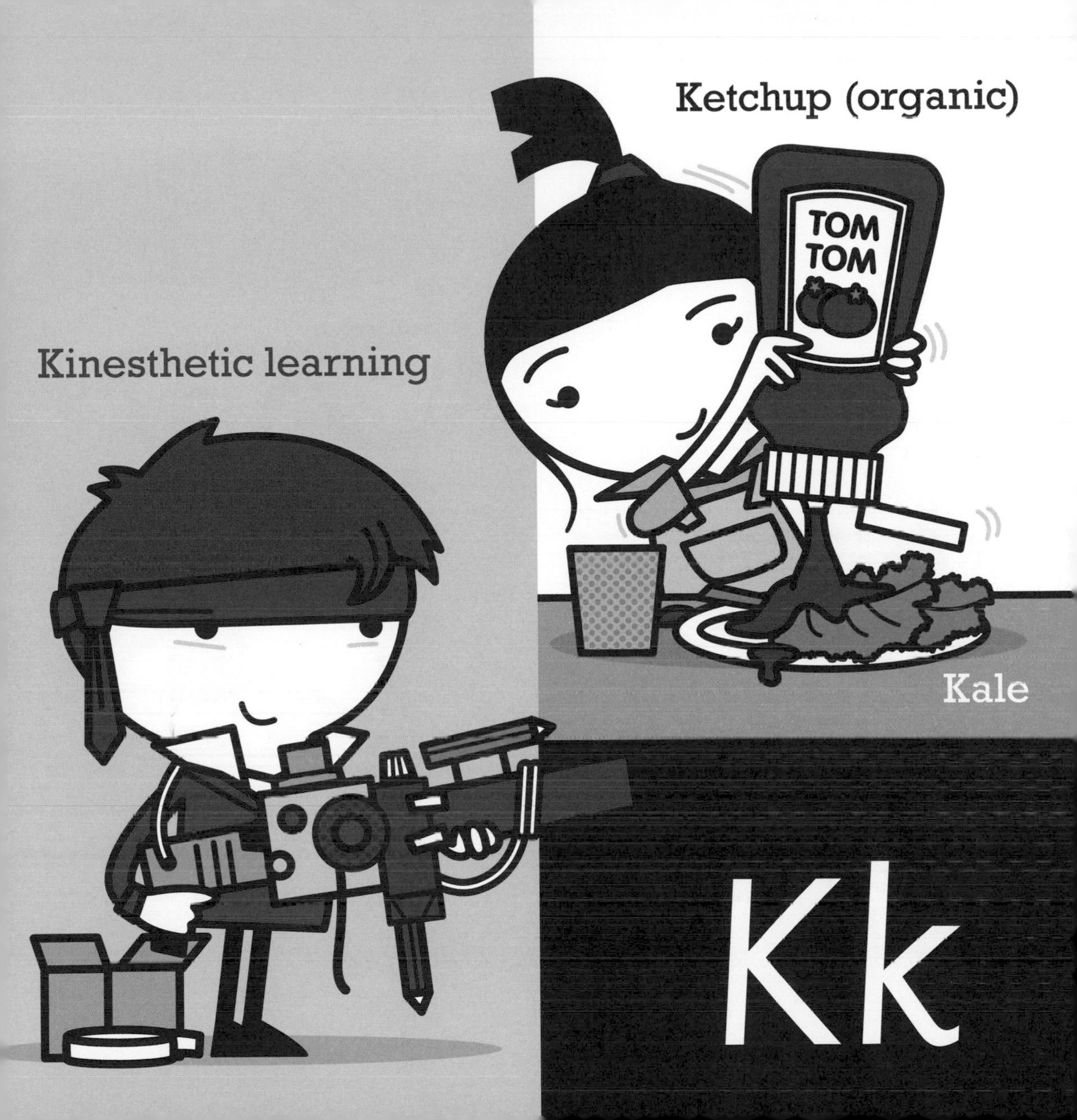
Ketchup (organic)
TOM
TOM
Kinesthetic learning
Kale
Kk

Legos

Lactose deficient

Latching on

MILK

Ll

Mm

Moses basket

Muslin

Nn

Naughty step

Nanny cam

No!

Night feed

OCD
(Obsessive compulsive disorder)

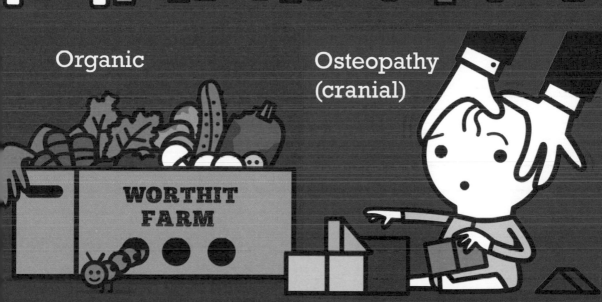

Organic

Osteopathy
(cranial)

WORTHIT
FARM

Pp

Projectile

Playdate

Mush

Puree

Pump and dump

Qq

Quinoa

Regifting

TO:
~~Ethan~~
Luca

Reward chart

Rr

Recycling

Rice cakes

Ss

Swaddle

Snot Sucker

SUV

DONT WALK
WALK

Soft play

Tt

Tiger mom

Tylenol

Unreasonable

Vaccination

Uggs

Uu

Ultrasound

Vv

Visual stimulation

Vitamins

VITSTERS
They're Chewy!

Violin lessons

Ww

Wine time

Wheat intolerant

Xanax

Xx

Yy

Yogurt
(probiotic)

Yummy mummy

Joel Rickett

is a publisher and a (very) occasional writer.
His previous books include *How to Avoid Huge Ships* and *Whitstable Mum in Custard Shortage*. He lives in north London, where he's a thoroughly modern parent to two gorgeous, demanding girls.

GONE
TO
LUNCH

Spencer Wilson

is an illustrator and co-founder of the illustration, design and
animation company Peepshow Collective. He has been drawing
since 1998 in a world of coffee cups and ordered chaos; his work follows this theme
with the creation of sketchy ideas and twisted thoughts. He lives in the modern
parenting paradise that is Berkhamsted, near London, with his wife
and two girls, who never cease to inspire him.

www.spencerwilson.co.uk   www.peepshow.org.uk   www.snydernewyork.com

This edition first published in hardcover in the United States in 2014 by

The Overlook Press, Peter Mayer Publishers, Inc.
141 Wooster Street
New York, NY 10012
www.overlookpress.com
For bulk and special sales, please contact sales@overlookny.com, or write us at the above address.

First published in the UK by Viking 2013

Cataloging-in-Publication Data available from the Library of Congress

Set in Rockwell, Sasson and Frutiger
Designed by Spencer Wilson
Printed in China

ISBN: 978–1–4683-0973-7

2 4 6 8 10 9 7 5 3 1